FORWARD

Two creative people living and working together can pose many challenges, but somehow, my wife Margee and I have made it work for several decades. The credit largely belongs to her, as she was blessed with some facility for organization that I am lacking, and lots of patience. Over those years we have worked hard to establish a life that both feeds our bodies and makes room for the creative endeavors that feed our souls.

The project, *In Tandem* mirrors our life as a couple in many ways. We went about this the way we often do, with Margee taking the lead and me procrastinating. Eventually, after some prodding from her, I would kick into gear and get moving, taking the lead, while she, not coasting, did however, slow her efforts. As we progressed, Margee asked if I had any ideas for a name for our project. I thought about our process of working together, and realized we were like a couple riding a bicycle built for two—   "In Tandem."

I have been a poet, writer, singer/songwriter for much of my adult life, and more recently, a painter. Margee, (although a fine writer in her own right) has primarily made her mark through painting and teaching the craft. After some urging from her, I took up oil painting myself few years ago, and joined her class. I might add, I am the teacher's pet.

Margee and I had been saying for, awhile, how cool it would be to collaborate on a project, that would bring together our artistic skills, but we weren't exactly sure what that might look like. In the midst of thinking about how we might work together on something, Margee received a call for proposals from Tulsa Artists Coalition. This created more urgency to come up with a plan.

We realized that after many years of marriage, raising two sons, restoring an old home, and with our various creative endeavors, we had a lifetime of collaboration already under our belts. We have a history of relying on one another for feedback on songs, poems, and paintings that are in progress. This would come in handy with our proposal for a show of painting inspired poetry and poetry inspired painting.

As we began to flesh out what that show might look like, we shared our idea with a friend who informed us that there is a word for this sort of collaboration. It is called "ekphrasis." We didn't think it could hurt to have a fancy Greek name included in our proposal and to our delight; our project was accepted, and so began the work on "In Tandem."

Now we would have the opportunity to be more intentional about our collaboration, Margee, with visual art, and I, the written word. Our original plan was to find poems that might inspire Margee to paint and paintings that would inspire me to write a poem. Several pieces in the show were created in this way; *Cecil, Beautiful Poison, Remembering Albuquerque*, to name a few.

We discovered an interesting thing during the process. I tend to write poetry that deals with human emotions, memories, relationships, and which often includes people from my past who are no longer living. Margee leans towards representational work involving the natural world and living humans painted from life. Bringing the two together has been a challenge, but a fun one.

Early on we found that using a shared experience to spark a creative response was our preferred way to work. Several pieces were created in this way, including *Bone Pond/ Winter Day at Candy Creek* and *We Walk/ Walk into Fall,* and *Blessing of the Fields.*

When we visited a friend who is now a cloistered nun in France, we stayed at a convent guest house and were invited to participate in an annual blessing of the vineyards, orchards and gardens. The sisters lead us around the property chanting and singing in a language with which we were unfamiliar, yet struck us both as very beautiful. Margee captured the experience in a painting, and I later worked from memory and her painting to come up with the poem *Blessing of the Fields*.

We also scheduled times to work together. The poem, *We Walk.,* and the painting, *Walking into Fall* were the result of a weekend retreat with the intended purpose of being in nature together to seek inspiration. Our hope was that we would return home with a poem and a painting, which we did.

Like many creative endeavors, mystery often hides in plain sight, an angel dancing on the razors edge of our periphery. This was true for us, when we realized that three separate events converged to create the poem *Bone Pond*, and the painting entitled *Winter Day at Candy Creek*.

The original version of *Bone Pond* was written in 2008 after a hike on the Candy Creek Conservation Reserve and was, in my estimation, unfinished. It had some interesting images, but I had always felt I was grasping for something just out of reach.

Winter Day At Candy Creek was a plein aire painting Margee completed on a hike we took at Candy Creek, one week prior to my having a heart attack in 2012. At some point during my recovery from the heart attack, I revisited *Bone Pond* and mysteriously the poem, like what often happens with the creative process, took on a life of its own and went a direction I could never have predicted, any more than one can predict, say, a heart attack. A poem that was incomplete became whole in an instant. Margee wanted to include her oil sketch after remembering that she had painted it the week before I entered the emergency room.

The process of putting this show together has been a lot of fun and at times, difficult. We have thrown out a poem and a painting or two along the way. We have experimented, stepped out of the bounds of our comfort zones, encouraged each other and offered honest criticism. Most of all we relished the opportunity to create something together that we hope will be both beautiful and honest.

Note:
Paintings that correspond to poems, *This Stone* and *Dirt Roads on an Arkansas Summer Night* were created by Scott Aycock. All other paintings were painted by Margaret Aycock.

CLIMBING TREES

Summer's best for climbing trees.

A boy ascends sweet canopies—
a cool retreat spares summer's heat—
a challenge, too, to arms and feet,
to climb so high, to limit's reach.

A boy will risk,
both life and limb,
having steeled himself
on jungle gym.

For in that tree
tests mettles worth--
reaching boughs
highest berth.
Looking down
from lofty perch,
he laughs at cheating
death's dark hearse.

And boy and tree, agree—
find much affinity.
Their trunks, both
long and lean—
his back, strong,
like a beam;
for climbing trees—
and reaching dreams.

And reach he will,
over many years—
some dreams fulfill,
some disappear.

In age, he will close his eyes against the dark
and feel the rush
of hands on bark,
still climbing further
than limbs can trust.

And in an instant
all returns—
tall oak trees
and summer sun.

Everything possible,
once again—
like climbing trees,
and reaching limbs.

CECIL

Cecil keeps our yard trim as a sailor's beard-
not a blade of grass out of place.
With a surveyor's eye he places poles along
the hedge row,
making Grandma's English Boxwoods
level as poured cement,
stretching the length of the drive.

He starts early and works through, into the
heat of the day.
I am just a boy.
Cecil comes to back door, hat in hand, like a child asking a favor of a man.
"Mr. Jo Eddie's grandson, you 'spose I could have me some 'freshment?"
I go under sink where grandma keeps the
drink, pour comfort from a bottle.
I place a capful in a glass, fill the rest with water.
It turns the color of rosin.

That'll do, Mr. Jo Eddie's grandson, don't need no ice.
He tips his head, tosses the drink, and wipes
his mouth.
It is a litany of motion.

Five drinks into the day, his tools put away,
Cecil comes to the door- a final drink to stay
the blues away.

I being home alone,
Cecil points with fingered bone
towards ivories lined up in a row.
"Mr. Jo Eddie's grandson, I can make that
coffin sing.
Some folks they scared a dyin', but they ain't got that rhythm thang."

Cecil straddles piano bench, with one leg north, the other east,
to work the pedals, to keep the beat.
With both hands poised on whitened keys,
his long black fingers fill spaces,
make dark holes in the music,
as he begins a slow growl, a low moan.
"How…how…how…uh…uh…unh.
Gonna' chase those blues.
How…how…how…uh…uh…unh.
Gonna' chase those blues."

Bowed over the keys, eyes closed,
Cecil is there in some sepia-toned place.

It seems with every note, with every chord,
Cecil spills more of himself between the keys,
as though the music is drinking him one note
at a time.

With an ear bent to the ivories, listening for the sound of suffering
as it leaves his fingertips;
Cecil's hand begins to jitter, and juke, and then to jive,
into some boogie-woogie slide.

His huge black hands, like crows,
flap the width of the piano,
as Cecil tosses back his head, enraptured.

I am just a boy held in time.
Watching.

As Cecil's shoulders sway in time to the beat,
mouth open, he eats.

Drinking notes, swallowing chords,
half-digested they come spilling forth,
crude and primitive.
A truer sound.

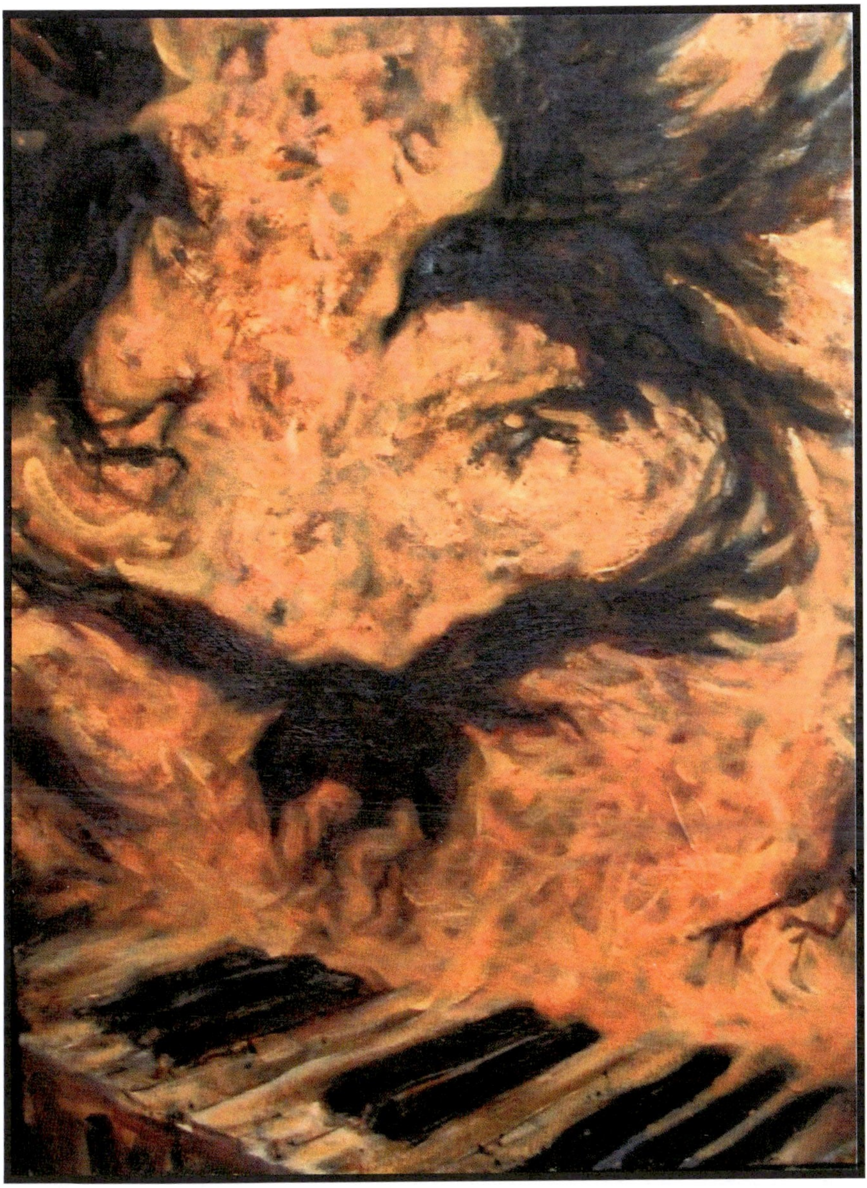

WE WALK

My lover and I are on retreat—
a cabin in the woods.

Leaving behind cell phones, and computers—
we walk.

The path is wide, clearly marked—
no getting lost.

We feel at ease on this unfamiliar path,
whereas, back home, in the city
familiarity seeds boredom,
and yes, sometimes resignation.
Trodden paths turn to ruts,
roots are exposed,
like fingers pointing.
We are lost.

For now, though,
in tandem,
we walk.
me in front
and then pausing
to observe a mushroom,
or catch my breath,
she will take the lead.

Out here, cooperation, not competition,
rules the day.
I offer a hand crossing a creek,
and stopping to rest,
she offers me water and a smile.

Still we are cautious, but curious.
New trails are like that,
only a hint of what lies ahead.
We walk.

It is mid-September and already,
the sun sits lower in the sky.
Slant light is warm, almost hot,
as the trail steers us into one of the many grassy clearings.

On this high plane
we walk
among blue stem, cacti, and crimson-crowned sumac.

The path gives way and dips into deep shadows.

I stop before wading into
       Pine—
              Oak—
                     Juniper.
She steps beside me,
her arm brushes mine.

Standing there, she whispers,
"Can you feel it? It's like leaving summer and walking into fall."

True, the heat gives way abruptly.
Cool moist air rushes up the descending path.
Stepping under the canopy
there is a hushed silence.
Instinctively, I reach for her hand and
we walk.

REMEMBERING ALBUQUERQUE

Standing before pinyon peaks,
Turquoise light of a New Mexican dawn
yawns over the earth.

I remember

A child's heart leaps as heat, dust, and clay
gathers on the flat-line-horizon
of an Arkansas summer day;
A mirage of mountain.

I remember

Mother, Father
stretch the bounds of your love
between two poles.
Drags the wounded child
from Sandia to sandy loam.
A trail of tears.

I remember

He wears his shame like ashes
smeared across his face.
With the onset of darkness,
he paints himself the colors of rage.
Angry at the loss of place.

I remember

Standing shadowed by Sandias,
Scent of sage and cedar
permeating my skin,
only then can I claim memory.

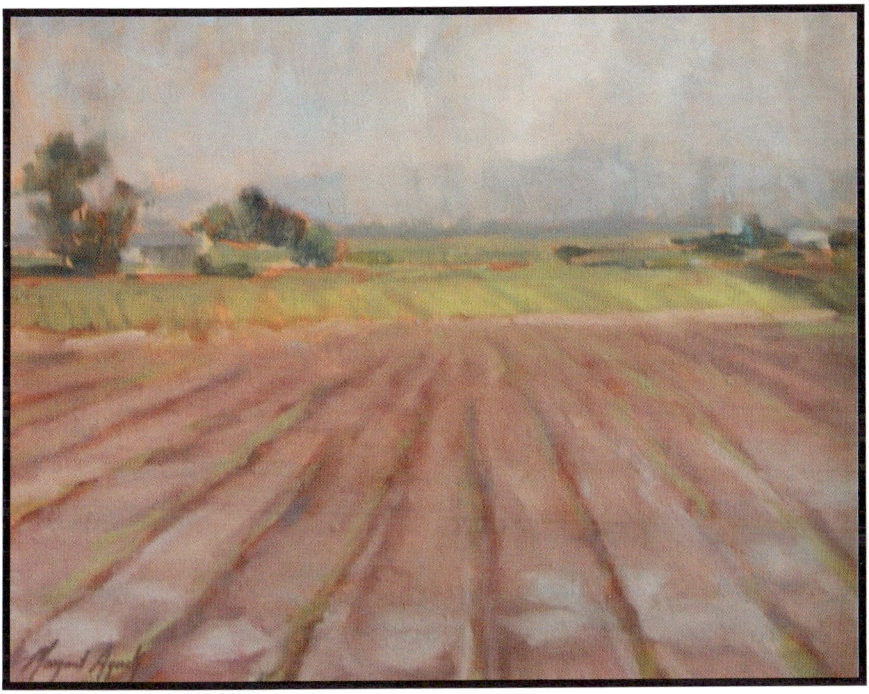

SHARED SPACE

The plastic cowboy
on the plastic horse,
rides across my windowsill.
He is at home,
sharing space
    with shells,
        rocks,
            and marbles.

I have him next to a Prince Albert Tin,
too confining a space for a prince, if you ask me.

I live in shared space,
charged molecules,
rubbing shoulders with humanity.
Nothing static-
    Changing,
        challenging,
            charged.
I am rarely at home in this space.

I read the paper this morning –
Woman in bikini thong
douses herself in gasoline-
burns for world peace.

It is shared space.

A gay man is murdered by a man
he confessed to loving on national tv.

Shared space.

A madman orders
the genocide of a whole people.
My country orders
the death of the madman.

Shared space.

Albeit, an uneasy space,
like breathing underwater –

plenty to drink in,
little room for air.

Looking again at the cowboy,
he seems poised,
ready at any moment
to crash through the window pane,
riding off, into the sunset.
Perhaps he's not so comfortable,
after all.

POEM FOR A HUNTER
(for Ben)

"Your name, Benjamin, of the tribe of Benjamin,
'Son of Thy Right Hand.'
The name of a warrior who serves a good and just king."

Coming into my life at a time when I was lost in the wilderness of pre-adolescence,
you were the solid oak I could climb to get my bearing.

A hunter, in the woods you are most at ease,
as though you were born out of time and place,
cut from the same buckskin as Daniel Boone.
In those woods, with you, I am safe.

Unsettling to me are
fleeting shadows,
    unfamiliar sounds,
        unusual markings in the ground.
You understand the signs, this is your language.

You press on through dense thickets,
wade shallow bayous, creep along a draw or
belly-crawl a sage and cacti dotted prairie.
I follow, knowing
as long as I can see and hear you, I will not be lost.

In the woods the rules are simple—
stay close,
    know where the other person is at all times,
        leave the safety in lock position, until you are ready to shoot,
            and lastly, never fire at anything you can't see clearly.

Navigating the world away from the woods was harder—
the rules more complex, the markers difficult to interpret.

You did not fully understand the tangled emotional territory
of a child separated from his father.
I had not the skills to mark the trail,
making it all the more difficult.

We both stumbled through internal, unmarked terrain.
Sometimes shots were fired carelessly.
Often we hesitated, not knowing if the safety was on or off.

That is behind us now.
Older, we are more comfortable,
having shed many skins.

Less encumbered, your dreams soar with owl and nighthawk.
In your hunter's dream you run with—
wolf
  deer,
    and buffalo.

In my dreams,
I am with you,
running too.

When we grow tired,
we sit by a still pool.
I look at you and see
that you hold the wisdom
gathered from listening in the silence
to whispered secrets of deep woods--ancient woods.

The lines on your face remind me
of all the many paths taken that have led
to this place.

DIRT ROADS ON AN ARKANSAS SUMMER NIGHT

Fishtailing along gravel and then dirt roads on an Arkansas summer night,
we drove fast.

We were young and had all the time in the world.

Somewhere inside our still unblemished, wrinkle-free bodies,
behind our bright burning eyes, the lamps to our souls,
we knew.
Knew that youth would not be available to us
in endless supply.

We were young and had all the time in the world.

We had seen the expiration date stamped in the furrowed brows of our
parents.
Observed the road map of age spots and blue veins,
through translucent skin of grandparents, like blue highways
we would travel.

We were young and had all the time in the world.

Weekends were a caravan of cars, circling Dairy Queens and the Piggly Wiggly
parking lot,
in an endless stream of self-consciousness.

We circled wagons to keep the illusion we were safe from the passage of time.

We were young and had all the time in the world.

 Sometimes, a car would break free, like a meteor leaving its orbit, and tear
down back roads, the place we felt most alive.
No destination, just the next curve, next rise, the next . . .

We were young and had all the time in the world.

Often there would be the near miss, the deer, the road that suddenly dead
ends, the too soft shoulder, and the oncoming car on the too narrow road.
We were left high on the rush of our blood, and the quickened beat of our
hearts.
Our collective breaths caught and then expelled as one single prayer of relief.

We were young and had all the time in the world.

We did not know then what we would come to know later,
that near misses would mean the missed career, the almost love affair, the child that nearly was, the endless dreams we could not hold.

We were young and had all the time in the world.

For now, though, under a clear a spray of stars, on this Arkansas summer night,
the night is young, we are young, and the road is waiting.

We have all the time in the world.

WOMAN IS A RIVER

Woman is a river wet and flowing responsive yet unchanging the slightest stroke of a finger
skimming her surface will cause her to ripple should I plunge a finger deeper she will part briefly to receive only to wrap her wetness around should I step boldly into her current she will spread wide and heave against my body enveloping me with all the force and passion she can bring threatening to sweep me up with her lift me from the mooring of solid ground resistance is futile and to surrender is terrifying it is this place we find ourselves when caught up in this current of rippling flesh lost but afraid of losing surrendered but fearing surrender caught between ourselves and another wanting to be wine and vessel and neither to immerse ourselves wholly into another is a baptism where if we surface we are born again should we not surface and instead lose ourselves drowning in the deep mystery of her inner thighs going deeper past pink folds of swollen flesh deeper still into the wet inner chamber that echoes the pulsing heart a heart that urges us to go deeper further like a whirlpool we are sucked under struggling to hold on to some imaginary limb or rope until flailing we are at last without resistance and there is only the sweetest surrender.

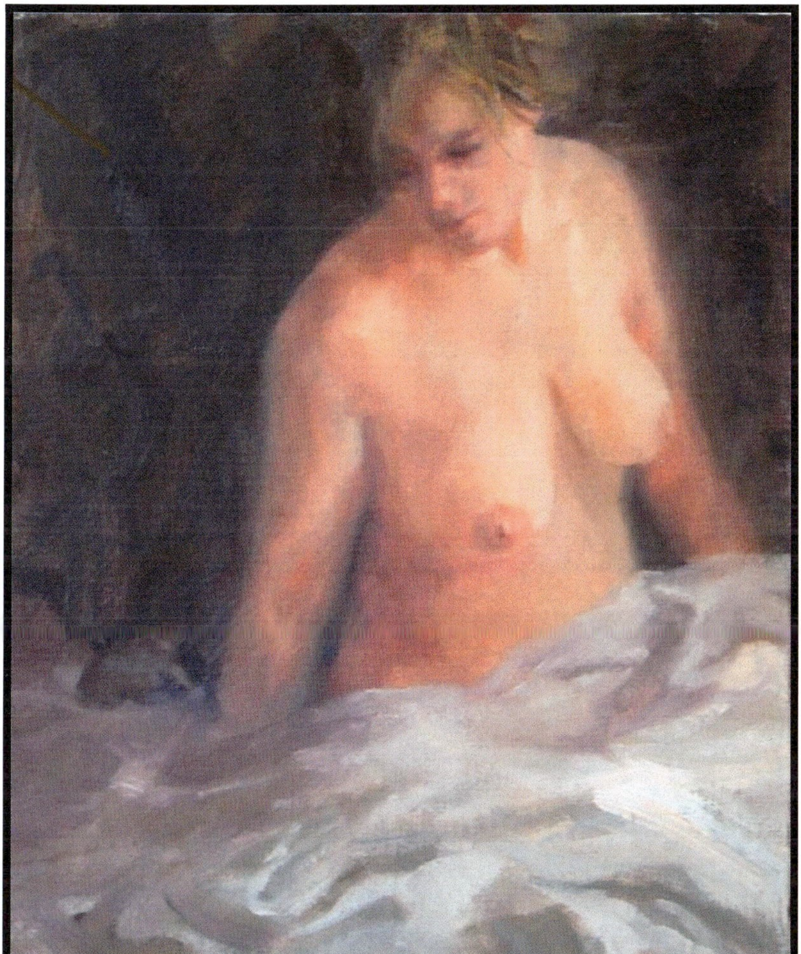

SPRAY OF CARDINALS

Looking out my window to the backyard,
cup of coffee in hand,
winter apple tree, for an instant, seems ripe with fruit.

It is a desire for the return of spring that brings on this illusion.

Closer examination reveals
cardinals scattered among the branches.

Their crimson silhouettes,
stand, most brilliant against the bleak, washed sky.

For months, I have looked out on this scene--
    Grey sky,
        grey fence,
            grey branches.

Rooftops of neighboring houses are degrees of grey.

My eyes now, weary of grey, are delighted by this late winter offering.

I become aware that I am cupping my coffee in both hands,
as though receiving Eucharist.

Then, in a flash of red, the tree ignites in winged flight.

Startled, I blink, and everything is the same again, only different.

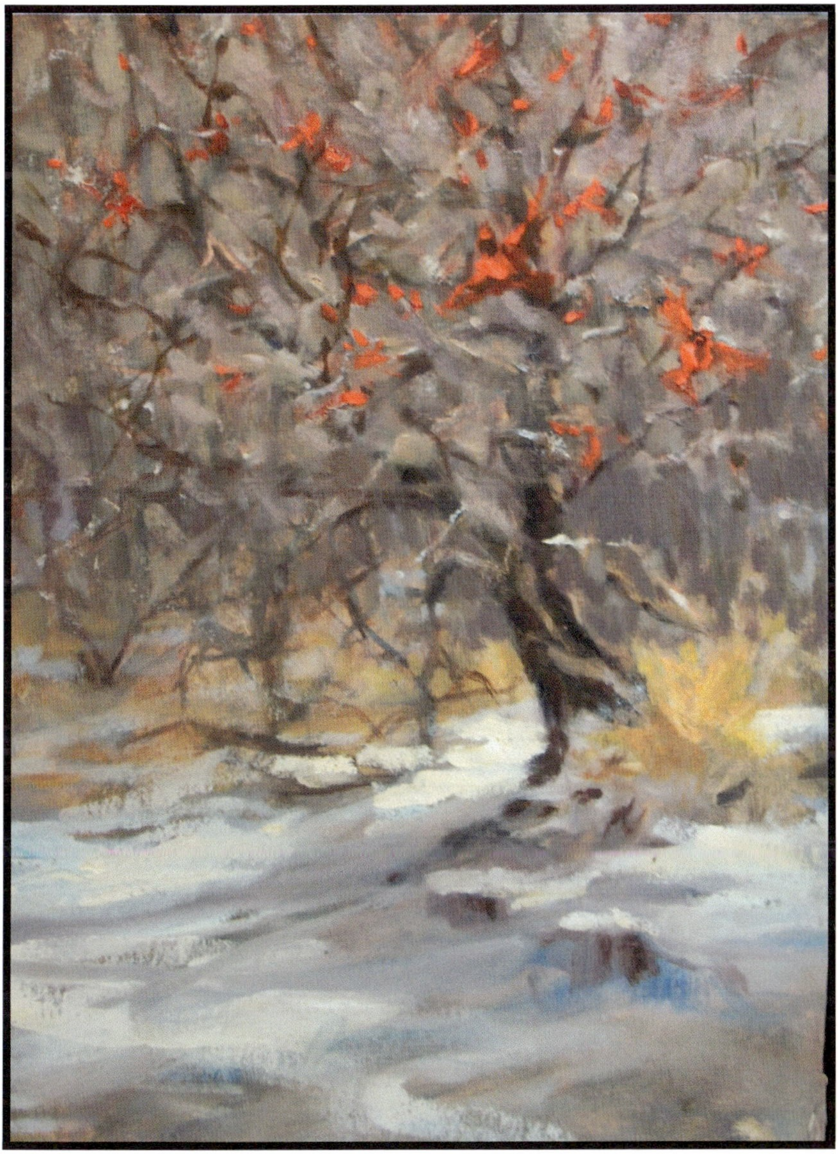

BONE POND

Walking the woods today
I stumble on to a repository of bones
in a dry pond bed-
proof of teeming life only months earlier.
Summer drought created this graveyard.

A multitude of animal tracks criss-cross
like some primitive game of tic-tac-toe
between amphibians, reptiles, and mammals,
wherein the winner manages to survive a little longer.

Letting go all other instincts in their quest for water,
they put away hunger.
The desire to reproduce becomes a whisper.

Walking the perimeter of this dry, shallow pond the ground is cracked and uneven,
Forming thousands of jigsaw puzzle pieces; stepping stones in a sacred labyrinth.

I walk, in ever-tightening concentric circles,
contemplating the primal urge to live and the shortness of life.

I place my palm to my chest and feel the steady beat.
Only months earlier, my own drought;
river of blood stopped flowing, yet,
the doctor said my heart kept beating-
"for nineteen minutes it beat," he said.

In remembering back to that moment
Past and future do not exist.
Time is measured in breaths.

Only after survival
does meaning assert itself.
People say, "Bet that was a wake-up call."

"From what?" I wonder. "Have I not been awake?"

Others assert, "You will be more grateful from now on."

Always implied, is that I wasn't grateful enough, as though more gratitude would have prevented what happened.

Bending to pick up a perfectly formed skull,
a coyote, or maybe a fox.
I hold it in my palm and stare
into hollowed out spaces
that once were eyes.

It becomes clear to me that, among all these scattered bones there lies no truth, no great meaning.

Looking around, I see no patterns,
just random piles of bones
lying here and there,
like a game of pick-up sticks.

When faced with survival,
there's nothing that is sacred-
not life, not death.
Still, holding this skull,
I can imagine his dull eyes,
his ragged breath,
his thirsty, swollen tongue
lapping the ground, the air
for a drop of moisture.
There is no tomorrow, no yesterday.
There is only this.

 Startled by this thought,
I realize I have been holding my breath.
Breathing deeply, I feel my lungs expand,
my tee shirt draw tight
across my chest.
I smell the hint of rain.

BEAUTIFUL POISON

Moonflower opens to the heavens
as daylight is shed from the earth.
Its name so appropriate, with blooms the color of moonlight.

A scent thick and dreamy is exhaled into the night air,
sweet and seductive.

Can one trust a flower that hides in the light of day,
folds into itself like a love note that no one can see, only to spread itself,
shamelessly at night,
welcoming, inviting all to her charms.

I am told that every inch of her is poisonous,
not to be trusted.

Some call her jimson weed,
and I am reminded of gypsies in the night,
come to steal away our babies.

Romantic and mysterious gypsies.
Gypsies twirling,
long pleated skirts opening like flowers to the moonlight.
Such a beautiful poison.

She sits across from me on the balcony.
A full moon frames her face.
She smiles an offering, as she reaches her wine glass towards my lips.

I hesitate, then nervously recover,
grab my own glass and tap it to hers.
"A toast," I proclaim.
She seems confused and a little bothered.
"To the moonlight."

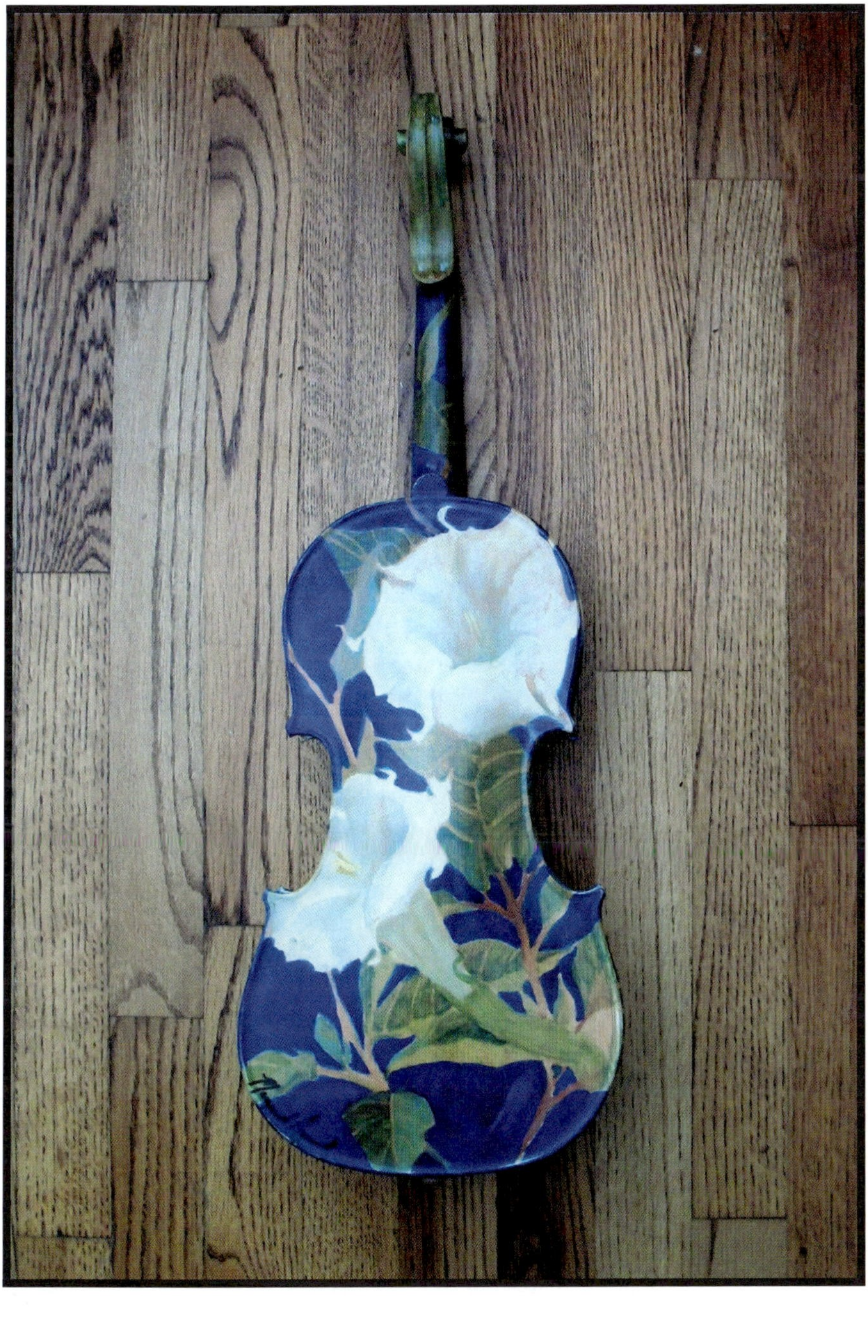

OLD ROSES IN A VASE

Sitting at the kitchen table,
old roses in a vase—
flower heads bowed over
like they're saying grace.

They've been there on the table
for two weeks or maybe more—
ever since you kissed me
and walked out that door.

How was I to know
you were never coming home?
How was I to know?
How was I
to know?

I remember the morning
I turned the TV on—
watched the buildings burn,
watched the towers fall.

You were in the building—
you called me on the phone,
told me that you loved me—
then you were gone.

How was I to know
you were never coming home?
How was I to know?
How was I
to know?

I know I will move on someday,
and put the roses in the cedar chest—
where I keep some things to remind me
of how you were the best.
There is our wedding picture—
the one of us at the beach.
There's that bowl I always got for you—
that you could never reach.

How was I to know
you were never coming home?

How was I to know?
How was I
to know?

Goodnight my love—
I will try to get some sleep.
I picture those poor roses,
as they bend their heads to weep.

Maybe I will dream of you
and maybe I won't.
Either way makes no difference—
for this is my love note.

Blessing Of The Fields
(Written after a visit to Notre Dame De Fidelity in France)

Already a week has passed at the Abby,
and I a stranger, taken in by good Samaritans,
have watched as nuns skit about in pairs or small groupings,
and sometimes alone—
always they seem to be forward leaning,
as though their eyes see further than the horizon,
something hidden from the rest of us.

With great intention they go about their earthly tasks,
    Cooking—
        Cleaning—
            Plowing—
                Seeding—
No separation between heaven and earth,
    Praying—
        Chanting—
           Serving—
                Singing—
God is in the mundane and the holy.

Nuns gather outside the Abby
by the fence row like
a murder of crows.
They are sister crows,
black gowns ruffling in the breeze.

Folded head to toe in black,
there could be the suggestion of something sinister afoot,
but not so with these sister crows—

For as I watch them bow and exchange joyful glances
in anticipation of the blessing of the fields, I admire them,
so clearly of one mind and heart,
united in this one good thing.
After-all, what could be more important to crows, than a blessing of the fields?

I am rarely of one mind,
two minds at odds on a good day.

The nuns shuffle about unencumbered,

as though their robes were flesh.
Far more comfortable are they in their skin, than I, in mine.

They file out,
one... by... one...
beads on a rosary.

Today I am both observer and participant.
I am invited to enter in.
These spirit guides lead the way.

I follow behind,
as they walk the circumference of the field,
chanting in a tongue foreign to me.
Their voices take flight upward and I am with them, circling the fields.
I too, see beyond the horizon.
The earth, in all its abundance spreads before me,
and the sky... oh, the sky... endless,
world without end.

No longer observer only,
I see fields awash in light and shadow,
and crimson poppies where fields lie fallow,
and something shiny under olive tree,
a memory to take to nest with me.

RED RYDER RIFLE

I remember the day my brother
put down his Red Ryder Rifle.
"I'm too big for kid games," he said.

He stood, ducking his head,
exiting the door to our fort.

I pleaded, "Don't go,"
but my brother was through the door.
Then taunted,
"what's the matter- too big to play with me now?"
The voice of a child could not bring him back.

For my brother it was no longer a choice.
He shook off his childhood
as though the fit weren't right.

I watched as he strode 'cross uncle's pasture toward giggling girls
huddled at the gate,
speaking in whispers I could not understand.
My brother understood.

He walked stiffly,
his creased jeans barely breaking line.
It occurred to me, he walked like my father.

The door closed.
For a moment I was sad,
and then I remembered the Red Ryder Rifle.

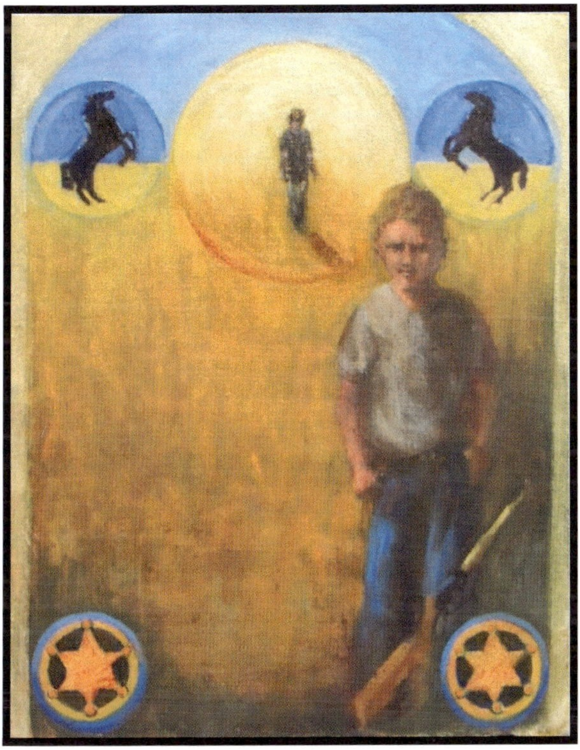

THIS STONE

Barely seven,
I followed behind Grandfather's plow,
scratching earth.
Cool, bare feet,
in fresh-turned dirt.

From where I stood,
all seven rows pointed to him.

Barely seven,
I followed behind.
Leapt over clods of clay,
scanning the tobacco-toned earth for a hint of color.

Unearthed, I plucked this fossil stone,
smelled its age, tasted its origin.

In my pocket
it became mine.

As a child
I did not know what my dreams knew,
that from where I stand today,
rows, like threads
would stretch far beyond my grandfather
to mountains, oceans, endless prairies,
and ever-changing skies;
stitching me in a tapestry of
death and birth,
    past and present,
        love and loss.

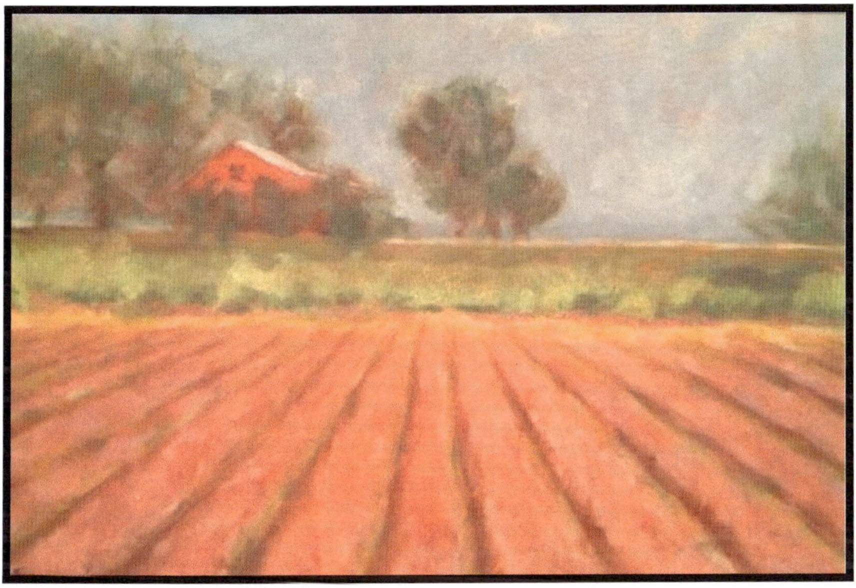

ODE TO THE DUSK

People, like fire, burn at both ends
until all that has been borrowed on this earth
turns to ash.

Smoke and spirit mix in the twilight of our lives,
and the warrior sings one more ode to the dusk,
lifting voice with the nighthawk and coyote,
crying out to the amber light and turquoise sky.

He paints himself the color of sunset.

Made in the USA
Charleston, SC
14 October 2015